WITHDRAWN

Managing Allegations Against Staff

personnel and child protection issues in schools

Maureen Cooper & Bev Curtis

Published by Network Educational Press Ltd.
PO Box 635
Stafford
ST16 1BF

First Published 2000
© Maureen Cooper and Bev Curtis 2000

ISBN 1 85539 072 8

Maureen Cooper and Bev Curtis assert the right to be
identified as the authors of this work.

Every effort has been made to contact copyright holders
and the Publishers apologise for any omissions, which
they will be pleased to rectify at the earliest opportunity.

Series Co-ordinator - Anat Arkin
Series Editor - Carol Etherington
Cover design by Neil Hawkins, Devine Design
Internal design and layout by Neil Gordon, Init Publishing

Printed in Great Britain by
Redwood Books, Trowbridge, Wilts.

CONTENTS

INTRODUCTION

A teacher or other member of the school staff will often be the first adult outside a child's immediate family to notice that the child is distressed, failing to develop or has non-accidental injuries. As a result, legislation has given school staff an important role in child protection. They are required to look out for signs of neglect and of sexual, physical and emotional child abuse.

The same daily contact with children that enables school employees to identify possible abuse by others also means that they themselves are vulnerable to accusations of abuse. Occasionally, an accusation turns out to be well founded.

In this handbook, we are not primarily concerned with the child protection procedures that are designed to protect children from abuse by people outside the school, such as relatives. While we do touch on these procedures, our main focus is on helping headteachers to manage the difficult personnel issues that arise from allegations against members of the school's own staff. We also look at the measures schools can take to ensure that the environment they provide for children is a safe one.

Like other titles in the EPM series, *Managing Allegations Against Staff* is aimed at headteachers, other senior managers in schools and members of the Governing Body's staffing committee. A short summary of the role of governors in managing child protection issues, particularly allegations against staff, is included for the benefit of other governors.

Maureen Cooper and Bev Curtis

The following icons are used throughout the book to identify certain types of information:

Case Study   Legal   Checklist   Model Procedure

CHAPTER I
REDUCING THE RISKS

Changing attitudes

 The idea that children need protection from abuse is a relatively modern one. Until 1889, children in Britain had no legal protection at all from abuse by parents and others responsible for their care. Legislation to protect children from sexual abuse by relatives took even longer to reach the statute books.

It was not until well into the twentieth century that the attitude that "an Englishman's home is his castle" began to give way to acceptance that there were occasions when the authorities needed to intervene in family life." Even then, teachers and care workers remained apparently above suspicion. In recent years, however, there has been a radical change in attitudes. A series of high profile scandals in children's homes in Cheshire, Merseyside, Cambridgeshire, North Wales and elsewhere has led to a recognition that sexual abuse of children is far more widespread than had previously been supposed, and that the culprits can include teachers and other professionals as well as relatives of the victims. While much of the spotlight has been on claims of sexual - and, to a lesser extent, physical - abuse at residential schools and care homes, there have also been well-publicised cases involving staff at non-residential schools.

Against this background, child protection issues now have a far higher profile in schools than they did in the past. Teachers and other school employees are expected to be alert to signs of abuse and to report any concerns they may have to a designated senior member of staff, often the headteacher. On an institutional level, schools are required to co-operate with local authority social services departments and other agencies involved in investigating allegations of child abuse.

It is also now recognised that school, like home, should be a safe place for children. All schools are therefore expected to have internal procedures for dealing with suspected abuse of pupils by members of staff. We consider these procedures in a later chapter. In this chapter, however, the focus is on what schools can do to reduce the risk of harm to their pupils.

Milestones on the road to a child-protective society

1883 - Foundation of the Liverpool Society for the Prevention of Cruelty to Children, the first British organisation to campaign against cruelty to children

1884 - The National (originally London) Society for the Prevention of Cruelty to Children (NSPCC) founded

1889 - The Prevention of Cruelty to and Protection of Children Act

1908 - The Punishment of Incest Act

1948 - The Children Act: led to the appointment of local authority children's officers

1989 - The Children Act: established the current child protection regime

1999 - The Protection of Children Act: designed to prevent paedophiles from working with children

Source: *The National Society for the Prevention of Cruelty to Children*

Setting standards

There is little schools can do to prevent family members and other people outside the school from abusing children physically, sexually or emotionally. There is, however, a great deal they can - and should - do to minimise the risk of abuse by members of the school's own staff, whether these be teachers or other employees who come into contact with pupils. In particular, schools are strongly advised to draw up a code of conduct governing relations between adults and children. By clearly setting out the standards of conduct expected of employees, this will not only offer children a measure of protection but also safeguard teachers and other school employees from the potentially devastating consequences of false allegations. A model code of conduct, which schools may adapt for their own use, is included in Appendix A of this book.

In drawing up a code of conduct and taking other steps to reduce risks to children, school managers need to consider the different kinds of behaviour that constitute abuse, and the situations in which abusive behaviour - or the appearance of it - might occur. We consider some of these below.

Danger zones

One of the characteristics of sexual abuse is that it takes place in private. Therefore, members of staff should not have the opportunity to create private spaces for themselves within the school.

Music practice rooms can easily be turned into private places since they are small, sound-proofed and often found in out-of-the-way parts of the school. Other potential danger zones include the caretaker's store cupboards and offices. It is not unusual for the caretaker to be only person with keys to these spaces, as there is usually very little reason for other members of staff to enter them. Similarly, technicians' store cupboards or preparation rooms are often tucked away in remote corners of the school that see very little through traffic.

The staff who use these out-of-the-way spaces may sometimes turn them into private recreational areas, complete with easy chairs and refreshment facilities. While their intentions may be wholly innocent, it is unwise to allow employees to use any space in this way without the authority of the headteacher or other senior member of staff. Managers need to have an overview of how all of the accommodation within a school is used and to make sure that no member of staff has sole access to any room or large storage area. They also need to watch out for - and put a stop to - any form of voyeurism.

Voyeurism: a checklist of behaviour to watch out for

The following types of behaviour can be associated with voyeurism:
- excessive visits to pupils' PE changing rooms;
- allowing poor discipline, including teasing and horseplay, in changing rooms;
- staring at pupils, particularly girls;
- finding excuses to get pupils to bend over, for example by dropping items;
- standing too close to pupils;
- turning a blind eye to pupils downloading inappropriate material from the Internet.

Grooming behaviour

Child sex abusers devote considerable time and energy to 'grooming' their intended victims. This involves deliberately setting out to win children's trust, sometimes over several years, before actual abuse occurs.

In some cases, the potential abuser will forge links with a pupil's family, perhaps by giving the child a regular lift home or by visiting the home under the pretext of providing extra help with school work. By winning the family's trust in these ways, the abuser will gain greater access and power over the child.

While strong home-school links can have a positive impact on children's development and academic progress, school managers need to let all staff know that out-of-school contacts with pupils and their families do have their dangers. Even where the member of staff concerned has no intention of harming a child, such contacts can give rise to the appearance of inappropriate behaviour.

Unlike actual sexual abuse, the grooming of victims occasionally takes place in the classroom, where a teacher may seek to win the trust of a group of children, perhaps by sharing apparently innocuous 'secrets' with them. This kind of situation is most likely to arise in schools that allow classrooms to become the private domains of individual teachers. Managers can create a more open culture by using regular classroom observation to monitor teachers' performance and by introducing the practice of staff observing each others' teaching.

Blackmail

A secondary school PE teacher exhibited typical grooming behaviour when he picked out girls who showed some aptitude for sport and volunteered to give them one-to-one coaching. He invited them into school at weekends and, by devoting time to them and flattering them, created a climate of trust which he soon began to abuse. This began as a 'joke', when he would stand at the only exit to a particular room and refuse to let the girls leave until they had given him a kiss on the cheek.

Gradually, as a targeted girl became more vulnerable to him, he would demand more than kisses. If a girl objected, she would be dropped, but one girl in particular responded to being described as 'special' and 'a woman', and so he was able to develop the relationship into a sexual one. Because the interior of the room was not visible from the outside and there were never many people in the school at weekends, he was able to pursue this abusive relationship for a long period. It stopped only when a parent eventually complained to the police.

The abuse might have come to light much earlier, or perhaps not have occurred at all, if the teacher's head of department or other senior manager had been alert to the danger signs and questioned why these particular pupils needed one-to-one coaching out of school hours.

Private meetings

A certain amount of one-to-one contact between pupils and teachers is unavoidable in a school, for example for music practice, special needs work or careers interviews. Senior staff with responsibility for timetabling need to ensure that these contacts do not take place in remote areas of the school or at times when no-one else is around and that, wherever possible, the door to the room being used is kept open. Half-glazed doors that make the interior of rooms visible from the outside are recommended and staff should be discouraged from covering up the glass with notices, posters or displays of pupils' work.

Private meetings between teachers and individual pupils should not be arranged off the school premises without the prior approval of the headteacher or another designated senior member of staff. Staff should also be strongly discouraged from offering lifts to children in their cars, except when this is an organised arrangement, for example to transport pupils to a sports fixture. In such cases, managers should ensure that the necessary insurance arrangements have been made and that no pupil travels alone in a car with a member of staff.

Out-of-school and after-school activities

Sports fixtures, concerts, and other out-of-school activities, especially residential visits, all represent potential dangers. While a relaxed atmosphere can contribute to the success of these activities, it can also encourage inappropriate behaviour or behaviour that might be misinterpreted by young people. Employees need to understand that they are expected to maintain the same high standards of professional conduct when supervising pupils in out-of-school activities as they do in the classroom. This is especially important in relation to younger members of staff.

The school outing

Sandra Kelly had just turned 16 when she was suspended for unruly behaviour from the school that she had attended for the previous five years. Although she was not expected to return to the school, she was invited to the end-of-year school journey to the seaside.

Rumours of an inappropriately close relationship between Sandra and her maths teacher, Andrew Leighton, had long been circulating around the school. However, since neither Sandra nor her foster parents had ever complained, Mr Leighton had escaped investigation. His headteacher had counselled him against spending too much time with the girl, but had not taken the rumours seriously.

On the day of the school outing, Sandra and Mr Leighton soon managed to wander off on their own. They walked along the beach and, when they were some distance from the rest of the party, sat down in a sheltered spot on the sand. Not realising that Janet Hague, a classroom assistant, could clearly see them from a nearby sand dune where she was supervising a group of pupils, they began kissing and cuddling. To Mrs Hague's amazement, they then partially undressed and appeared to have sexual intercourse.

The next day, Mrs Hague reported what she had seen to the school's headteacher. Mr Leighton was suspended from his post pending a hearing before the dismissal committee of the school's Governing Body. The headteacher also informed the police of what had happened. They were not able to take any action against Mr Leighton because Sandra was above the age of consent and insisted that she had had sexual intercourse with her teacher willingly. At the time, there was no criminal sanction against people abusing a position of trust in the way that Mr Leighton had done.

At his dismissal hearing, Mr Leighton claimed that he had done nothing wrong because Sandra had been suspended from the school, and was no longer his pupil at the time of the alleged offence. He also emphasised that he had never acted improperly on school premises and that what he did outside school was his own affair. This line of argument did not impress the members of the dismissal committee, who were particularly concerned that the teacher had abused his position of trust in relation to the girl. They recommended his immediate dismissal for gross misconduct. The chair of governors also instigated disciplinary proceedings against the school's headteacher for failing to investigate the earlier allegations against Mr Leighton. These proceedings ended in a first written warning to the head.

Newly-qualified teachers

Newly-qualified teachers are often only three or four years older than their sixth-form students, and will need direct guidance on how to form appropriate relationships with students. This should be included in the induction training for newly-qualified teachers, and should aim to help them to understand the dangers of socialising with students, particularly in situations where alcohol may involved.

 It is now an offence for an adult who is in a position of trust to engage in any sexual activity with a young person aged 16-18 (see Chapter 2). However, the law is always a blunt instrument when it comes to regulating people's behaviour and, rather than waiting until an offence has been committed, schools need to ensure that young teachers are aware of what constitutes acceptable behaviour in relation to pupils, especially those who are close to them in age.

Physical contact

Physical contact, such as an arm around the shoulders, may be acceptable when an adult is comforting a child in distress. However, some children dislike being touched, while adolescents may misinterpret any kind of physical contact. Cultural background will also determine what is and is not acceptable to an individual child. Adults therefore need to be sensitive to children's reactions, their age and background, and adjust their behaviour accordingly. They also need to be very careful not to touch children in ways that might be viewed as inappropriate or indecent.

Physical contact is sometimes unavoidable in the context of physical education, drama teaching and some forms of skills coaching, but such activities must not be used as an excuse for touching pupils. Teachers themselves can often demonstrate particular techniques without touching pupils and, to avoid misunderstandings, contact should not be used unless there is clearly no alternative.

Bullying

Bullying is always unacceptable, whether the perpetrator is an adult or a child. Defined as 'deliberately hurtful behaviour', it can take many forms, including name calling, publicly or privately humiliating people, spreading rumours about them and excluding them from group activities. Repeated bullying of a child by a teacher or other adult in authority constitutes emotional abuse, and can damage the child permanently.

Just as all schools need to have a policy on bullying by pupils, they should also give teachers and other members of staff guidance on what constitutes bullying in relation to their own behaviour. This can be included in the code of conduct for staff and in induction training for newly-qualified teachers.

Emotional abusers often have strong personalities and a network of allies who will stand up for them. Since they rarely abuse children in front of other adults, their behaviour can be difficult to detect. Those who intimidate children with sarcastic, belittling comments are even harder to identify than those who resort to open verbal abuse. None of these difficulties should be allowed to deflect headteachers from tackling emotional abuse in the same way as any other kind of abuse. On the other hand, heads need to recognise that it is not unknown for a parent or a group of parents to make unsubstantiated allegations of emotional abuse against a particular member of staff.

Aches and pains

The parents of a six-year-old became worried when their son developed mysterious stomach aches and did not want to go to school. The child claimed that his teacher was 'picking' on him, holding his work up to ridicule in front of other children and making sarcastic comments about his dress and appearance.

The teacher denied these allegations and pointed out that six-year-olds tell tales and often cannot distinguish between fact and fantasy. The school's head observed a few of the teacher's lessons and found nothing untoward in her behaviour towards pupils, though the pupils did seem unusually submissive or over-eager to please in their response to the teacher. However, when several other parents, including two who had clearly had no contact with each other, made similar complaints, the head concluded that there was substance to the allegations.

Threatened with formal disciplinary action, the teacher admitted that she had sometimes been "slightly impatient" with the children. She eventually agreed to leave the school under a compromise agreement. (See Chapter 3 of this book and also Chapter 3 of *Managing Poor Performance,* another handbook in this series.)

Sex and relationship education

Under education law, governors are responsible for deciding whether to include education about sexual abuse in the curriculum. However, there is a requirement for schools to have a sex and relationship education policy.

Teaching young children about the risks of abuse and how to avoid it may help them to remain safe. However, it can also undermine normal relationships with adults and encourage children to make false allegations. Therefore, any education on sexual abuse should be approached with extreme sensitivity and pitched at a level appropriate to children's age and maturity. It is best to use staff who have received specialist training in this area, although all teachers involved in a school's personal, social and health education programme will need to cover sex and relationship issues.

Primary school children

As the age of sexual maturity falls, primary schools need to take the same kinds of precautions as secondary schools in relation to supervising out-of-school activities or one-to-one contacts between pupils and staff. Primary school teachers also need to take care that their words and actions are not misinterpreted by sexually precocious children.

Staff appointments

Schools obviously need to do all they can to avoid appointing people who have abused children in the past. DfEE circular number 9/93, *Protection of children - disclosure of criminal background of those with access to children* updates earlier guidelines on arrangements for checking the possible criminal backgrounds of people applying to work in schools. Searches are made by the Criminal Records Bureau.

To qualify for a police check, posts have to involve 'a substantial level of access to children, which may also be unsupervised, and will be regular or sustained'. One-to-one contact with a child is normally regarded as 'substantial', even if it lasts only for short periods. On the other hand, a classroom assistant, for instance, who spends long periods of time around children but is always under supervision, would not normally be regarded as having 'substantial access'.

Checking for possible criminal backgrounds

Schools should make sure that police checks have been carried out on the following categories of staff:

- teachers, including trainees on the graduate and registered teacher programmes;
- paid and unpaid classroom assistants;
- nursery nurses;
- caretakers and other site workers;
- school librarians and library assistants;
- laboratory and other technicians;
- sports instructors;
- residential care workers;
- escorts of vulnerable children;
- drivers of vehicles used to transport children without escorts.

If a person who comes into regular contact with children is not a school employee, the headteacher, acting on behalf of the school's governors, they should ensure that the individual's employer has requested a police check and that this has been carried out.

This will apply, for example, to:
- supply teachers employed by an external agency;
- educational welfare officers;
- educational psychologists;
- youth leaders.

Checks are not normally necessary for the following categories of staff, unless they have substantial unsupervised access to children:
- administrative staff;
- cleaners;
- catering staff;
- lunchtime assistants and supervisors;
- gardeners and grounds maintenance staff;
- parents and other supervised helpers;
- student teachers (except those on the graduate and registered teachers programme);
- other trainees (except in nursery schools).

All application forms should seek candidates' agreement to a police check, though a check will only be carried out if an application has been successful. Application forms should also include a notice requiring candidates to disclose whether they have ever been cautioned or convicted of a criminal offence.

A copy of this notice should be sent to the applicant's referees, who need to be informed that posts involving contact with children are exempt from the 1974 Rehabilitation of Offenders Act and that they should therefore reveal any information they may have concerning cautions or convictions which would otherwise be considered 'spent'. The notice to referees should also explain that any information they provide will be kept in strict confidence and used only to consider the suitability of the applicant for a post involving contact with children under 18.

It is up to the school's governors and headteacher to decide whether or not to employ someone who has a criminal record but has not been barred from working with children. Governors may take the view that a minor offence, perhaps committed while a candidate was very young, can be safely overlooked. On the other hand, they would be very unwise to employ someone with, for example, a history of violence.

Convictions or cautions for possession of cannabis can present governors with a quandary. While some may personally take the view that cannabis is harmless, they need to recognise that society is sharply divided on the issue and that, in child protection terms, employees who use drugs are seen as a risk to children. Therefore, governors should think carefully about appointing people with recent convictions or cautions for possessing drugs, especially to posts where they would have an influence on children and young people. As a rough rule of thumb, they should avoid employing anyone who committed a drug-related offence while employed in the education service.

List 99

The Secretary of State for Education and Employment has the power to bar an individual from employment as a teacher or worker with children or young persons, a category that includes school caretakers and care workers in special or residential schools.

Those convicted of sexual offences against children under the age of 16 are automatically barred from such employment. These offences include rape, buggery, indecent assault and taking or distributing indecent photographs. It is extremely unlikely that a school would want to employ anyone convicted of such offences, even if they did not involve children.

In other cases, the Secretary of State has discretionary power to bar an individual. The regulations do not set out an exhaustive list of the kinds of misconduct likely to lead to barring, but DfEE circular number 11/95, *Misconduct of Teachers and Workers with Children and Young Persons*, gives a number of examples, including a sexual offence against someone over the age of 16, drug trafficking and any offence involving serious violence.

List 99 contains the names, dates of birth and, where applicable, the teacher reference numbers of people barred from employment in maintained or non-maintained schools on medical grounds or because of misconduct. The Department of Health keeps a similar list of people who are unsuitable to work with children in the child care sector. Anyone included on this list is now also barred from employment in the education service. Before appointing a teacher or other employee who will come into contact with children, schools must first check (normally though their LEA or personnel adviser) that the individual's name does not appear either on List 99 or on the Department of Health's list.

A word of warning

Neither police checks nor the existence of lists of people barred from working with children should lull schools into a false sense of security. Child abusers tend to be very adept at hiding their activities and side-stepping systems designed to detect them. Schools cannot therefore be certain that a new member of staff with an apparently clean bill of health from the police and the DfEE represents no danger to children. A rigorously enforced code of conduct offers better protection, though this too will never be entirely foolproof. It is a regrettable fact of life that most headteachers will have to deal with allegations against members of staff at some stage in their careers.

CHAPTER 2
THE LEGAL
BACKGROUND

When there are grounds for suspecting that a teacher or other member of a school's staff is subjecting a child to physical, sexual or emotional abuse, the school has to take account not only of child protection legislation but also of employment and education law. Headteachers need to make sure that they have access to advice and information on developments in all three of these fast-changing areas. They should also be aware of the tensions that exist between the aims of child protection legislation on the one hand, and employment law on the other.

Child protection law

 The most important piece of legislation in relation to child protection is the Children Act 1989. This places a duty on local education authorities (LEAs) to work with social services departments that are investigating allegations of child abuse or acting on behalf of children 'in need' - defined as those who have been abused or are at risk of abuse. All LEA-maintained schools, including foundation schools, are indirectly subject to these provisions, which have also been extended to city technology colleges and independent schools, and further education and sixth-form colleges.

 ### Child protection procedures in schools

The practical implications of the Children Act for schools are set out in the DfEE circular number 10/95: *Protecting children from abuse: the role of the education service*. The circular's main points are summarised below:

- All school staff should be alert to signs of abuse and know where to report any concerns or suspicions they may have.

- Every school should have a designated member of staff responsible for co-ordinating action within the school, as well as liaising with other agencies, including the Area Child Protection Committee (ACPC). This individual should receive appropriate training.
- Schools should be aware of the child protection procedures established by the ACPC and, where applicable, by the LEA.
- Every school should have a procedure for handling suspected cases of abuse of pupils, including those that need to be followed if a member of staff is accused of abuse.

The guiding principle of the Children Act is that the child's welfare is paramount. This means that social services departments can intervene, for example to remove a child from the family home, by satisfying a court of law that the child is suffering or is at risk of suffering 'significant harm'. Actual harm to the child need not be proved so long as the relevant agency can show that there is a real risk of significant harm to the child at home, in school or anywhere else.

A further principle of the Act is that any delay in determining a question related to a child's upbringing will usually be considered likely to prejudice the child's welfare. In other words, social services departments and other agencies involved in child protection are required to act quickly and decisively when they have reasonable cause for suspecting that a child is suffering or is at risk of suffering ill-treatment or neglect. However, these agencies have no authority to suspend a school employee who is suspected of harming or intending to harm a child.

The Children Act gives the police considerable powers to intervene in suspected child abuse cases, including the power to remove a child to safe accommodation. The police may also, of course, start criminal proceedings where they have grounds for believing that an offence has been committed. Again, however, the police have no power to suspend or require the suspension of an individual from his or her employment. In schools, this power rests solely with the Governing Body and the headteacher.

In exercising this power, governors need to consider the provisions in education and employment law relating to staff disciplinary procedures and dismissal. Designed to protect the rights of employees to fair treatment at work, these provisions are in some ways at odds with the principles of the Children Act, which can lead to the tensions that we mentioned at the beginning of this chapter.

Employment law

Employment law recognises just five fair reasons for dismissal. These are:

- misconduct;
- lack of capability;
- statutory enactment;
- redundancy;
- some other substantial reason.

'Statutory enactment' covers those situations where an employer cannot legally continue to employ an individual. An example relevant to schools would be where it is found that an employee has been barred from working with children and young people. 'Some other substantial reason' usually applies to people in senior posts, for example where school governors have lost confidence in a headteacher's ability to protect children, and believe that continuing to employ that individual could put children's safety at risk. In most cases of physical, sexual or emotional abuse of children by school employees (including those that amount to 'gross misconduct') dismissal would be for 'misconduct'.

Governing Bodies need to be very clear about their reasons for dismissing an employee because an employment tribunal will judge the fairness of a dismissal in relation to the reasons given for it. So, while governors may wish to avoid the bad publicity that cases of child abuse invariably attract, they should never submit to the temptation to give incompetence or redundancy as the ostensible reason for getting rid of an actual or suspected child abuser. If governors do give a reason that they cannot substantiate, the sacked employee could end up winning up to £50,000 in damages for unfair dismissal.

More seriously, an employee sacked on the grounds of redundancy or even incompetence may well find a new job in another school, whereas someone sacked for misconduct involving children would probably be barred from working with children or young people in future. It is important, therefore, that schools do not solve their own problems at the potential expense of other schools and their pupils. Under DfEE Circular 11/95, a member of staff who is dismissed or resigns to avoid dismissal for misconduct in relation to pupils should be reported to the Secretary of State.

In judging whether a dismissal is fair, an employment tribunal will consider whether the processes leading up to the decision to dismiss have been fair. This means that staff disciplinary procedures in schools have to comply not only with certain requirements laid down by education law, but also with the *Code of Practice on Disciplinary and Grievance Procedures* issued by the Advisory Conciliation and Arbitration Service (ACAS). While this code does not have the force of law, an employer's failure to follow ACAS advice may be admissible in evidence and will weigh in the employee's favour if the case reaches an employment tribunal.

Under the ACAS code, an employee accused of misconduct (other than gross misconduct) is in the first instance entitled to receive an appropriate warning. It is only if this warning fails to have the desired effect that further disciplinary procedures, including dismissal, will need to be invoked.

The stages of formal disciplinary procedures

In schools, a formal disciplinary procedure usually consists of five stages:

1. Recorded verbal warning (in some cases with a right of appeal).
2. First written warning (normally given by the headteacher), with a right of appeal as set out in the school's procedure.
3. Final written warning (normally given by the headteacher) with a right of appeal as set out in the school's procedure. (Under some procedures, decisions on final written warnings are made by a panel of governors, but we would recommend that disciplinary action up to and including such warnings are delegated to headteachers, with a right of appeal to the governors.)
4. Dismissal by the governors' dismissal committee.
5. Appeal against dismissal to the governors' appeals committee.

At each stage of the disciplinary process, the employee has the right to know what it is that he or she has been accused of doing, and to have the matter properly investigated.

Education law

 Successive education acts, culminating in the School Standards and Framework Act 1998, give Governing Bodies of maintained schools responsibility for managing teaching and non-teaching staff who are paid out of the school's budget. This includes responsibility for establishing disciplinary rules and procedures. Governing Bodies of foundation and voluntary-aided schools, which are described as 'maintained' in the 1998 Act, have similar responsibilities, though unlike community and voluntary-controlled schools, they need not inform the LEA of decisions to dismiss employees, unless they have given the authority advisory rights.

The Act also sets out the mechanisms for dismissing employees for misconduct, including gross misconduct, or for any of the four other lawful reasons. A staff dismissal committee, made up of at least three members of the school's Governing Body, has to hold a hearing to consider the allegations against the employee, who must be given the chance to reply to these allegations either directly or through a representative. The employee also has the right to appeal against dismissal to a separate staff appeal committee of the Governing Body, which must consist of governors who took no part in the original dismissal hearing and are therefore impartial.

This procedure has to be followed even when governors are considering the dismissal of an employee for gross misconduct, which can be defined as misconduct so serious that it makes an individual's continued employment unacceptable. Although gross misconduct justifies dismissal without any previous warning or notice, a school employee cannot lawfully be dismissed without a hearing before a committee of governors and the opportunity to appeal against that committee's decision. The dismissal does not come into effect until the appeal process has been exhausted, and the employee is entitled to remain on full pay until that happens, though in almost all cases the employee will be suspended pending this decision (see Chapter 3).

Gross misconduct and misconduct

Examples of gross misconduct involving children or young people include:

- physical violence towards pupils;
- sexual relations with pupils (whether they are under the age of consent or not);
- other sexual misconduct (for example, showing pornography to pupils);
- off-duty sexual misconduct, including sexual relations with children or young people other than the school's own pupils.

Examples of misconduct involving children or young people include:

- pushing, pulling or grabbing pupils;
- abusive or offensive language directed at pupils;
- forming inappropriate 'friendships' with pupils.

Staff disciplinary procedures and the law relating to dismissal are considered in more detail in another title in the Education Personnel Management Series, *Managing Challenging People*.

Other relevant legislation

The Human Rights Act

The rights of employees to fair treatment at work, already strengthened by the Employment Relations Act 1999, which reduced the qualifying period for protection from unfair dismissal from two years to one year, have been further reinforced by the Human Rights Act 1998. This came into force in October 2000, and gives effect to the European Convention on Human Rights. Whilst the Convention has long had an influence on UK law, and British citizens have for many years been able to take cases to the European Court of Human Rights, they are now able to enforce their rights in British courts. The Act requires public bodies, including the Governing Bodies of maintained schools, to act in accordance with the Convention, which guarantees individuals a number of basic rights. These include the right to a fair trial or hearing before 'an independent and impartial tribunal'.

In practical terms, this means that, when conducting disciplinary hearings, school governors must act fairly, and be seen to be acting fairly. So if, for example, the governors' dismissal committee refuses to allow an employee to make representations or call witnesses, an employment tribunal may conclude that the hearing has been unfair. As we have seen, employees are already entitled to a fair hearing when facing dismissal, but the Human Rights Act means that the courts and employment tribunals will view procedural irregularities even more seriously than they did in the past.

Abuse of trust

 The Sexual Offences (Amendment) Act 2000 was concerned primarily with lowering the age of consent for homosexuals to 16 in order to equalise it with the age of consent for heterosexuals, but there was also an intention to ensure that adults in positions of authority did not prey on vulnerable young people. This led to the creation of a new offence of 'abuse of trust'. This offence applies to any adult, male or female, who holds a position of trust in relation to a person aged 16-18 of either sex and engages in any sexual activity with that young person. As well as making it clear to staff that sexual relationships with older pupils are always inappropriate, a school's code of conduct needs to point out that such relationships are now unlawful.

Physical punishment

 The use of corporal punishment was outlawed in maintained schools by the Education (No2) Act 1986, and in independent schools by the School Standards and Framework Act 1998. If a teacher or other employee is suspected of using physical punishment which goes uncorrected by the school, it is likely that the police will be informed and local child protection procedures set in motion. It is very unlikely that any employee would be allowed to continue using physical punishment these days, since the school would know about after it had happened once. If an employee does hit a child, and school managers become aware of this, they are strongly advised to deal with the situation though the school's internal disciplinary procedures rather than calling on external agencies. As we have mentioned, child protection procedures exist to protect children from the 'significant harm' that tends to be associated with repeated abuse.

In advising schools to use their own disciplinary procedures to deal with less serious, one-off instances of violence, we are not suggesting that physical punishment is ever acceptable - far from it. Behaviour directed at pupils which is in any way violent should always incur disciplinary action and will in many cases amount to gross misconduct that ought to result in the employee's dismissal. However, where there is no evidence of the child having suffered significant harm, the multi-agency approach identified by child protection procedures is probably inappropriate and may end up causing the child more distress than the original incident.

The case study below suggests how school disciplinary procedures might be used to deal with a teacher who has struck a child in frustration or who has used some form of physical punishment.

A warning

The following is a transcript of part of an appeal against a first written warning for misconduct issued by the headteacher of Anytown Junior School.

Present at the hearing:

Ms Alicia Boateng, chair of the appeals panel
Mr James Ross, governor
Mrs Carole Hedges, governor
Mrs Marion Cope, personnel adviser
Mrs Lucy Turner, headteacher
Mr Nick Jones, teacher
Ms Harriet Steel, union representative

Mrs Cope: The purpose of today's hearing is for the panel to consider an appeal against the decision of Lucy Turner, the headteacher, to issue a first written warning to Mr Jones following a disciplinary hearing on Tuesday 10th May 2000. (She produces copies of the first written warning letter.)

You will see from the letter that the warning regarded Mr Jones' conduct towards Gary Locke and his admission that he had actually shaken the boy. I will now take you through the incidents of that day, the events that followed and recommend that you uphold Mrs Turner's decision to issue a first written warning. I now call Mrs Turner as a witness.

Mrs Turner, could you please tell the panel how the incident involving Gary Locke first came to your attention?

Mrs Turner: Mrs Locke, Gary's mother, came to see me and said that Mr Jones had shaken Gary. At first, she was incandescent with rage but then she burst into tears.

Mrs Cope: Have you had many dealings with Mrs Locke in the past?

Mrs Turner: Yes, she has often come to see me because her son has found it difficult to settle in the school. Things had begun to improve lately so I was very concerned to hear her allegation.

Mrs Cope: What action did you take with regard to the allegation?

Mrs Turner: I said I would investigate the matter immediately and get back to her. I then contacted you as the school's personnel adviser, and you suggested I should see Nick Jones as soon as possible.

Mrs Cope: What did you do next?

Mrs Turner: I went to find Nick and saw him in the car park as he was about to go home. I told him I wanted to have a word with him about what had happened that day. He began to explain, but I felt it was not appropriate to discuss such a serious matter in the car park, so I arranged to see him in my office the following day.

Mrs Cope: How did Mr Jones describe what had happened?

Mrs Turner: He said that Gary had been misbehaving all morning. Then, just as all the children were leaving the classroom for lunch, he saw Gary pulling another child's hair. He called Gary to the front of the room and gave the boy what he described as "a talking to underlined by a good old shake".

Mrs Cope: Did you take a note of what Mr Jones had said?

Mrs Turner: Yes, I took notes. I also asked Mr Jones to demonstrate what had happened.

Mrs Cope: Could you show us what you saw?

(Mrs Turner shakes Marion Cope to demonstrate how Mr Jones had shaken the eight-year-old Gary Locke.)

Mrs Cope: What was your reaction to that?

Mrs Turner: To my mind, it amounted to corporal punishment which is, of course, illegal, and it was against the school's own policy, which Mr Jones had helped to develop only last year.

Mrs Cope: I understand Mr Jones then gave you a written account of the incident. What view did you take of that?

Mrs Turner: I was worried that the incident would undermine all the hard work we had put into building a relationship with the parent and positively influencing Gary's behaviour. I was also extremely concerned that Nick described what he had done as "a standard warning to little terrors".

Mrs Cope: Is Gary "a little terror"?

Mrs Turner: He can be difficult, but he is not beyond the control of Nick Jones, who is a highly experienced teacher.

Mrs Cope: What was your next course of action?

Mrs Turner: As Nick wasn't denying what had happened, I requested a written statement from Gary's mother. Then, since the incident had been a breach of the school's policy, as well as the legislation banning corporal punishment, I called a disciplinary hearing...

Physical intervention

 While it is always unlawful to use violence as a form of punishment, there are occasions when teachers and other school employees may use 'reasonable force' to restrain or control pupils. These powers, which existed under common law, were clarified by Section 550A of the Education Act 1996. This allows staff to use reasonable force to prevent pupils from committing a crime, injuring themselves or others, damaging property or causing disruption. It applies to teachers and other staff who have been authorised by the school's headteacher to have charge or control of pupils.

Section 550A provides a legal defence against allegations of assault, provided the member of staff involved can show that he or she used only 'reasonable force' to restrain or control a pupil. If an unreasonable degree of force has been used, Section 550A offers no protection, and the employee may be charged with the common law offence of assault.

Unfortunately, there is no legal definition of 'reasonable force'. However, any degree of force is unreasonable in a situation that could be resolved without physical intervention. Where force is used, it should always be the minimum needed to achieve the required result. The circumstances that will determine whether the use of force is reasonable and the degree of force that may reasonably be used include the age, understanding and sex of the pupil(s) concerned and the seriousness of the incident.

The ambiguity of the term 'reasonable force' means that any member of staff who intervenes physically runs the risk of being accused of common assault. It is by no means unusual for parents to complain to the police if any force at all has been used to restrain or control their children. There are also physical dangers to the member of staff, and it is usually best to seek help from colleagues or the police before intervening physically, though this may not be possible in emergencies. The case of the London headteacher who was fatally stabbed while trying to protect a pupil from attack offers a tragic illustration of the potential dangers of physical intervention. It should be used only as a last resort.

CHAPTER 3
DEALING WITH ALLEGATIONS AGAINST STAFF

Most school staff are familiar with local child protection procedures and understand quite clearly how to deal with a situation where a child is at risk from a family member or some other person outside the school community. Where the suspected abuser is an employee of the school, the issues become more complicated. The headteacher needs to consider not only how child protection procedures will apply but also whether to invoke the school's staff disciplinary procedure.

These two sets of responsibilities do not always sit easily together. While schools have an obligation to safeguard the welfare and safety of children in their care, they are also obliged to respect the rights of employees to fair treatment. As we have said, social services departments and other child protection agencies have a duty to intervene when they have reasonable grounds for suspecting that a child may be in danger. Governing Bodies, on the other hand, cannot dismiss an employee or take other disciplinary action merely because they suspect wrongdoing; they can act only on the basis of evidence, which on the balance of probability demonstrates misconduct.

In some cases, allegations of abuse take years to surface, by which time evidence to support them may be difficult to find.

A question of proof

A woman in her twenties informed the police that as a schoolgirl she had been sexually abused by a group of men, one of whom was her science teacher. The teacher, who was still employed in the school that the woman had attended, was suspended while the police looked into her allegations.

The woman admitted that she was drunk at the time of the alleged abuse. Her evidence was therefore judged unreliable and, in the absence of any other evidence to support her allegations, the police decided not to bring criminal charges against the teacher she had accused.

Although the school was still obliged to pursue the matter as a disciplinary issue, in the absence of reliable evidence of misconduct, the teacher had no real case to answer. The governors lifted his suspension and, despite protests from local child protection officers, he continues to teach at the school.

Ground rules

The Department for Education and Employment's Circular 10/95, *Protecting children from abuse: the role of the education service* gives guidelines for dealing with allegations of child abuse against staff. This document stresses the seriousness of any abuse of a pupil by a teacher or other adult who holds a position of trust in a school. But it also warns of the potentially devastating consequences that false allegations can have on an innocent person's health and career. Therefore, schools need to follow good child protection practice, while at the same time seeking to minimise the damaging effects of false allegations. Headteachers should not attempt to perform this difficult balancing act on their own, but should take professional advice whenever serious allegations are made against staff.

The initial response to an allegation

 Any allegation against a member of staff needs to be taken seriously and should not be dismissed out of hand merely because it is made by a child. Nor should a teacher or other employee who hears a child's allegations against a colleague promise the child confidentiality. School managers need to impress on staff that all allegations of abuse, even the most seemingly trivial, have to be reported.

When someone has made an allegation, the headteacher or other member of staff who heard it should make a written note of what has been said. This needs to cover all the points raised by the person who made the allegation, and should be signed and dated.

The headteacher then needs to make some initial checks as quickly as possible to establish whether there is any substance in the allegations. This will usually mean checking with staff and pupils who may have information indicating the possibility of the alleged incident(s) having occurred. Parents should be informed if a child is to be interviewed.

Possible questions to ask at this stage include the following:

- Were the child or children and the member of staff actually in contact on the day in question or on any day near to that day?
- Were they alone at that time?

If the answers to these questions is categorically "no", then no further investigation may be necessary. However, if the answers suggest that the allegations need further investigation, the headteacher should seek professional advice from the school's personnel adviser and, if it is a community school, inform the LEA. In all but the most exceptional circumstances, for example where it is immediately clear that the allegation is false, the police should also be informed.

Confidentiality must be maintained at this stage so as not to prejudice any subsequent investigation or damage the reputation of the accused employee who is, of course, innocent until proved guilty.

In a case of alleged sexual abuse, the school should not inform the member of staff concerned without the agreement of the police. This may seem to go against the principles of natural justice, but it is a practice designed to ensure that suspects in child abuse cases are not given the chance to cover their tracks. The police will normally wish to investigate whether an allegation constitutes a criminal offence. The more serious the offence, the more important it is for the school to avoid any action that could prejudice the police investigation.

Deciding what to do next

 In consultation with the local authority's child protection officer, the police and the school's personnel adviser, the headteacher must now decide whether to refer the matter to child protection agencies in accordance with locally agreed procedures. Where it appears that a child is at risk, an immediate referral will have to be made.

If there are no reasonable grounds for suspecting child abuse, but it appears that the allegation was prompted by the employee's inappropriate behaviour, this will need to be dealt with under the school's disciplinary procedures. For example, a teacher who 'jokes' that they find a pupil attractive should be formally warned not to repeat such behaviour.

If child protection officers, the police, LEA advisers and the headteacher unanimously agree that the allegation against the member of staff is clearly without foundation, he or she should be informed that no further action will be taken either under child protection procedures or under the school's own disciplinary process. Meanwhile, the child protection agencies will consider whether somebody else might have abused the child.

Before laying the matter to rest, the headteacher will need to consider whether to offer the employee professional advice or counselling. This should aim both at helping the employee come to terms with what has happened, and to avoid behaviour, however innocent, that may be open to misinterpretation. The head will then need to monitor the situation to make sure that the member of staff has followed this advice. So if, for example, the allegation concerned a teacher's behaviour while giving a pupil a lift home in their car, the head, or perhaps the teacher's head of department, should make sure that no further lifts are offered to pupils. Ignoring this instruction could in itself constitute serious misconduct, even if no misbehaviour of any other kind had occurred.

External investigations

If the police and child protection agencies decide that the matter needs to be investigated further, there will usually be a strategy meeting to plan the next steps and to determine whether other pupils could also be at risk. The headteacher should attend this meeting, which will need to consider the welfare of the possibly wrongly accused employee, as well as the conduct of the investigation.

Once a child protection referral has been made, the headteacher must hand over all relevant information to the police. This will include the written note of the allegation itself and the record of the head's initial checks. Obviously, no-one in the school should tamper with any evidence.

At this stage, the headteacher should make sure that the pupil and the pupil's parents or guardian are informed of the police investigation. The head will also need to tell the chair of governors and the accused employee what is likely to happen next and what decision has been taken on thorny issue of suspension.

Suspension

 When the police launch an investigation into allegations of child abuse involving a school employee, they often 'require' that the individual concerned be suspended. In some cases, the head also comes under considerable pressure from the LEA and child protection agencies to suspend the employee.
However, none of these bodies have the right to invoke a suspension. We have already mentioned that the power to suspend a school employee rests with the headteacher and Governing Body, who may not delegate this power to any person or organisation outside the school. Only the Governing Body can lift a suspension. In a community or voluntary-controlled school, the LEA has to be informed of any suspension, and may offer the head and/or governors advice, but that is the extent of its involvement.

The decision to suspend a member of staff is probably one of the most difficult that any headteacher ever has to make. In law, suspension is a neutral act intended to protect the position of both the employer and the employee while an allegation is being investigated; it is not a disciplinary measure. In practice, however, suspension is rarely seen in those terms. People tend to think that there is "no smoke without fire", and a suspension often damages an individual's reputation irreparably, even where the allegation turns out to be without any foundation.

According to claims by some teacher unions, there has recently been a sharp increase in the number of false or malicious allegations made against teachers. Heightened awareness of parents' and pupils' rights, a decline in respect for teachers' authority and an increasingly litigious society have probably all contributed to this development. Certainly, we have come across families who are known to the police for threatening legal action as soon as a child receives so much as a reprimand from a teacher. While the police are obliged to look into any allegation however trivial it may seem, schools should avoid the knee-jerk reaction of automatic suspension.

Some LEAs advise schools to suspend a member of staff as soon as any kind of allegation involving sexual or physical misconduct with children is made. Other authorities advocate a more considered approach that takes into account the seriousness of the allegation. From an employment law perspective, an employer who automatically suspends a member of staff without taking into account the circumstances of the case may be held to be acting unfairly. Our advice is that schools should not allow themselves to be rushed into any action, and bear in mind that an employee can be suspended at any stage of an investigation if such action becomes warranted. There always has to be sufficient reason to suspend a member of staff.

A loss to the profession

The headteacher of a secondary school stepped in to break up a playground fight between two boys. Although he used the minimum amount of force needed to separate them, the parents of one of the boys complained to the police, who arrested the headteacher and charged him with assault.

On hearing what had happened, the school's chair of governors, rather than making her own enquiries to establish whether the allegation of assault had any substance, immediately suspended the head. Fortunately for him, several teachers and pupils had witnessed the incident and were able to tell the police that he had used only as much force as was needed to stop the fight and to prevent the two boys from injuring each other. However, it took several months for the police to take statements from all the witnesses and complete their investigation. Meanwhile, the headteacher, who had been released on bail, remained suspended and became clinically depressed.

The police eventually decided to drop the case, and the head returned to school for a short time before taking ill-health retirement at the age of 52. A committed and able headteacher, he might have continued working for several more years had his chair of governors not suspended him so precipitously.

When to suspend

Suspension will generally be appropriate where:

- the allegation is serious enough to amount to gross misconduct if found to be justified;
- children could be at risk if the accused employee were allowed to remain in their post;
- there is a possibility that the accused employee might otherwise attempt to interfere with the investigation.

When suspension is under consideration, the headteacher should invite the member of staff to an interview, informing him or her in advance that it is advisable to be accompanied by a union representative or friend. The head will need to explain that the interview is not a disciplinary hearing but is held for the purpose of considering a serious matter.

During the interview itself, the headteacher should inform the employee that an allegation has been made and that suspension is being considered. The employee should be allowed to make representations concerning the suspension and should be given a chance to think about his or her response. If, after hearing this response, the head decides that suspension is necessary, the employee should be told that he or she is suspended from duty on full pay. Written confirmation of this decision, giving reasons for the suspension, should be sent to the employee without delay.

Model letter confirming a suspension

Dear Mr Jackson,

Following our meeting today, at which you were accompanied by your union representative Mr Stephens, I am writing to confirm that you are suspended from your employment as head of the music department. This suspension is a neutral act intended to allow further investigation to take place into a serious complaint regarding your conduct.

The complaint is that on Tuesday 22nd September 2000 you:

1) repeatedly touched a Year 7 pupil on the hands, arms and shoulders during the course of a piano lesson;
2) you then stood across the door of the music practice room, preventing the boy's exit and causing him considerable distress.

The police and the local authority's child protection team have been informed of the allegation, and may decide to pursue their own investigations. You will remain suspended on full pay pending the completion of any such investigations. Once the police have completed their enquiries, the school will conduct its own investigation into your conduct. If this reveals grounds for holding a disciplinary hearing before the staff dismissal committee of the Governing Body, you will be given 10 days' notice of the date and time of the hearing.

Should the dismissal committee find that the complaint against you is justified, you may be dismissed without notice for gross misconduct.

Yours sincerely,
A.M. Singh
Headteacher

Confidentiality

Where a member of staff has been suspended, the headteacher must inform the chair of governors of the reasons. The head should also let the Governing Body as a whole know that a member of staff has been suspended, but without going into any detail that might prejudice the position of governors involved in any subsequent hearing or appeal.

While some senior members of staff will have to be told of the reasons for the suspension, it is advisable to provide information only on a need-to-know basis. It is sometimes difficult, however, to 'keep the lid' on information about serious misconduct involving pupils, and the extent to which confidentiality can or should be maintained will depend on the circumstances of the particular case. In some cases, the head will need to reassure some or all parents about the safety of their children, as well as keeping them up-to-date with developments as the various investigations progress. The LEA's education welfare service and the local child protection team may be able to help to deal with the concerns of parents or staff.

Internal investigations

Investigations by the police or child protection agencies take precedence over all other investigations. This means that any internal investigation into allegations against a member of staff has to be put on hold while the police and child protection agencies pursue their enquiries. An internal investigation should not normally run alongside these enquiries.

Once the external investigation has ended and any child protection issues have been resolved, the headteacher will need to look at the facts of the case and decide whether to take disciplinary action against the employee concerned. That may involve interviewing the parents or pupils who made the allegation and making a written record of their statements. Occasionally, the police will agree to give the school statements already made to them, but this will need the consent of the authors of the statements. The school should take care how it uses such statements, since they were initially made for a different purpose.

When taking statements from children, headteachers need to make careful preparations in order to make sure that they do not miss out any important questions. Young children will not be able to make written statements on their own and should therefore be interviewed. Older pupils should write their own statements as soon as possible, before memories of the alleged event have faded. If a number pupils claim to have witnessed the event, speed in taking their statements is also crucial in order to prevent collusion.

The accused employee will also need to be interviewed and should be offered the opportunity to be accompanied. He or she should be told of the allegation and invited to respond, one should be offered the opportunity to be accompanied but cannot be required to make a statement. A note should be made of the interview and a copy given to the employee to sign as a true record. The employee should also have a chance to name people who might be able to provide information relevant to the investigation. These individuals should also be interviewed.

Once all of the interviews have been completed and the relevant facts gathered, the headteacher, in consultation with the chair of governors, will need to decide whether disciplinary action is appropriate. This decision should then be conveyed, normally by letter, to the employee.

Disciplinary action

If, as a result of the school's investigation, new information comes to light that makes a further child protection referral necessary, disciplinary proceedings will again need to be put on ice pending the outcome of further external investigations. If there is no new information, the school's usual disciplinary procedure should be allowed to take its course.

While there is no essential difference in the procedures that need to be followed in cases of alleged misconduct involving pupils and other types of alleged misconduct, there is a difficulty when it comes to calling pupils as witnesses. It is a basic principle of natural justice that the accused should know who the accuser is and have the opportunity to question that person directly. A denial of this opportunity could be construed as a breach of the employee's rights under the Human Rights Act (see Chapter 2). Nevertheless, it is often inappropriate to allow children to face their alleged abuser.

If pupils are not called as witnesses, and normally every attempt should be made to avoid doing so, it is very important to ensure that statements are taken from children very carefully, and in the company of a parent or guardian. The person who took the statement could then act as a witness at any hearing.

Occasionally, an older pupil may be called as a witness. Where this happens, it may be sensible for a parent, social worker or another teacher to accompany the pupil, particularly if the allegations are of a sexual nature. The room in which the hearing is held can be arranged in such a way that there is no direct visual communication between the pupil and the accused employee (see the diagram overleaf).

Layout of a room used to hear allegations by pupils

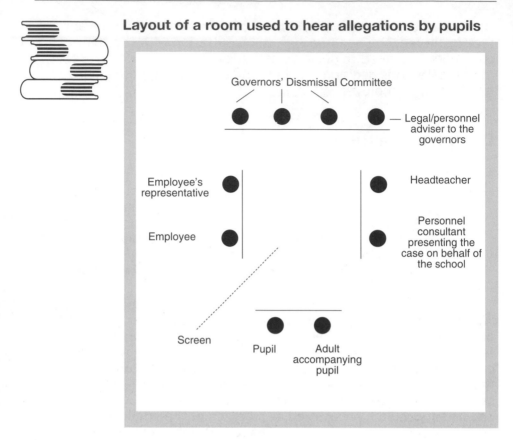

Record keeping

Schools need to retain documents relating to any external and internal investigations, together with a written record of the outcome of these investigations. The outcomes of any disciplinary action taken against a member of staff should also be retained on that individual's confidential file.

A potential difficulty concerns record keeping in cases that end in a formal warning to the employee, rather than in dismissal. ACAS recommends that warnings should normally expire after a year, but it is important to comply with the time limits in the school's own procedure. Where children's safety is at issue, there is an argument that warnings should remain on the employee's file for much longer, possibly indefinitely.

What headteachers should never do is to remove the warning from the official file after a year but keep a confidential record of it elsewhere. Under the Data Protection Act, employees are entitled to inspect their personal records, whether these are kept in computerised or manual files. If they find that information about them has been tucked away in the head's personal 'hit list' file, for example, they may have a legitimate grievance against the head. In any case, the school cannot reasonably act on a 'spent' warning, for example when giving a reference to a potential new employer. So, rather than attempt to get around data protection legislation, it is sensible for schools to state in their disciplinary procedures that, where child protection issues are involved, warnings will remain in force for longer than the usual 12 months.

Where a headteacher and the relevant child protection agencies decide that an allegation against a member of staff does not warrant any further investigation, all records of the allegation should be destroyed. Again, it would be poor practice - and possibly actionable - to keep a secret record of the allegation "just to be on the safe side".

Dismissals and compromise agreements

 If a member of staff is dismissed or resigns before the disciplinary process has run its course, the Governing Body has a statutory duty to report the case to the Secretary of State. As we have already mentioned, the Secretary of State may then decide to include the employee's name on List 99.

It sometimes happens that an employee is cleared of all charges of child abuse but finds that his or her position in the school has become untenable, perhaps because parents remain suspicious. In these cases, a compromise agreement may offer both the employer and an employee the only way out of a very difficult position.

A compromise agreement should not be used to 'hide' allegations of abuse.

The contents of a compromise agreement

A compromise agreement will usually include the following terms:

- The employee agrees to leave his or her post in return for an agreed sum of compensation.
- In exchange for this compensation, the employee agrees not to bring a claim for unfair dismissal.
- The headteacher undertakes to provide potential employers with an agreed reference. Any oral references need to be consistent with this written reference.
- The parties to the agreement agree not to make disparaging statements about each other and to keep the terms of the agreement confidential.

Handling media interest

Any school dealing with an allegation of misconduct against a teacher or other member of staff is likely to find itself at the centre of media interest. Journalists will usually steer clear of cases that are still *sub judice* for fear of being held in contempt of court, but once legal proceedings have ended or the police have decided not to charge the employee with a criminal offence, the gloves will come off.

Lurid headlines can cause lasting damage to a school's reputation, and some headteachers and governors respond to unwelcome media interest by 'battening down the hatches' and refusing to speak to reporters. However, this approach will not make the problem go away and could be counter-productive. If the headteacher or chair of governors will not talk to journalists, other people almost certainly will, often anonymously. Any school in this position would therefore be well advised to give its own side of the story by issuing a straightforward, factual statement. An example is given opposite.

Model press statement

Following an allegation against Mr Albert Jackson, former head of music at this school, the Countyshire Constabulary carried out an extensive investigation and decided not to charge him with a criminal offence.

However, the school's own internal enquiry into Mr Jackson's conduct did reveal serious grounds for concern. Mr Jackson is therefore no longer employed by the school.

The headteacher and chair of governors wish to reassure parents and members of the local community that this school demands the highest possible standards of professional conduct from all its staff. As Ofsted inspectors noted in their highly favourable report on the school last year, these standards are met in the overwhelming majority of cases. However, the school is never complacent about matters relating to the welfare of pupils, and plans to heed the important lessons that have been learnt from recent events.

For further information, contact the headteacher, Mr A.M. Singh, or the chair of governors, Mrs Mary McDonald, on telephone number 01234 567890.

A prepared statement will not always be enough to satisfy the media. Therefore, staff who answer the school's phone need to be told to expect calls from journalists, and to refer these to the head or chair of governors. They in turn need to anticipate the questions they might be asked and think of possible responses. After reading the above model statement, for example, journalists would perhaps ask why the police had decided not to press charges, what Mr Jackson did that led to his dismissal and what the school was planning to do to make sure "recent events" were not repeated. While total frankness may be inadvisable, a helpful attitude to reporters is likely to result in fairer press coverage than a "no comment" approach.

Every local authority has a press or public relations office which will be able to advise LEA-maintained schools on dealing with the media at times of crisis. Alternatively, or where no LEA is involved, schools could seek advice from private sector consultants specialising in media relations.

Allegations against members of staff - a flow chart of the stages

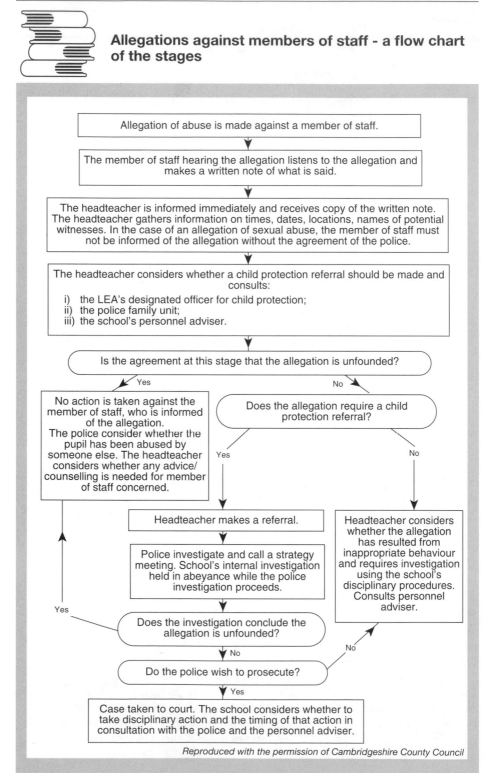

Allegation of abuse is made against a member of staff.

The member of staff hearing the allegation listens to the allegation and makes a written note of what is said.

The headteacher is informed immediately and receives copy of the written note. The headteacher gathers information on times, dates, locations, names of potential witnesses. In the case of an allegation of sexual abuse, the member of staff must not be informed of the allegation without the agreement of the police.

The headteacher considers whether a child protection referral should be made and consults:
i)   the LEA's designated officer for child protection;
ii) the police family unit;
iii) the school's personnel adviser.

Is the agreement at this stage that the allegation is unfounded?

Yes — No action is taken against the member of staff, who is informed of the allegation. The police consider whether the pupil has been abused by someone else. The headteacher considers whether any advice/ counselling is needed for member of staff concerned.

No — Does the allegation require a child protection referral?

Yes — Headteacher makes a referral.

Police investigate and call a strategy meeting. School's internal investigation held in abeyance while the police investigation proceeds.

No — Headteacher considers whether the allegation has resulted from inappropriate behaviour and requires investigation using the school's disciplinary procedures. Consults personnel adviser.

Does the investigation conclude the allegation is unfounded?

Yes

No — Do the police wish to prosecute?

No

Yes — Case taken to court. The school considers whether to take disciplinary action and the timing of that action in consultation with the police and the personnel adviser.

Reproduced with the permission of Cambridgeshire County Council

CHAPTER 4
DEALING WITH ALLEGATIONS - A CASE STUDY

Following a successful school production of *A Midsummer Night's Dream*, a distraught parent came to see Sue Willis, the head of Year 11. Mr Mahmoud claimed that his daughter, Sameha, who had been involved backstage in the production, had been "sexually abused" by her drama teacher, Ian Best. Brandishing a locket that Mr Best had allegedly given to his daughter, the angry father accused the school of being no better than a brothel, and said that if the drama teacher was not sacked on the spot, he would make sure those who had allowed the abuse to take place would be punished. He then broke down, saying his daughter would now not be able to find a suitable husband within the strict Muslim community to which the family belonged.

Sue Willis attempted to calm Mr Mahmoud down. She asked him for details of the alleged abuse and, after making a note of what he said, she promised to report the matter to the headteacher straight away and get back to Mr Mahmoud at the earliest possible opportunity.

On receiving the note, the headteacher, Peter Allen, immediately called Sameha Mahmoud into his office, where the tearful girl told her story, adding that she knew of at least one other girl - Jenny Oakley - who had also been kissed and "touched up" by Mr Best. The head asked Sameha and Jenny for written statements of what had happened, and talked to a number of other pupils who had been involved in the school play. He also spoke to Sue Willis and the parents of both girls.

These enquiries convinced Peter Allen that there was enough substance in the allegations to warrant further investigation. He therefore informed the chair of governors of the allegations, and contacted the LEA's designated child protection officer, the local constabulary's family unit and the school's personnel adviser. A strategy meeting was held. Since the allegation concerned inappropriate behaviour rather than a criminal offence, it was agreed that, initially at least, the matter would be handled via the school's disciplinary procedure. The police officer present at the meeting asked to be kept informed of developments and said her force would intervene if further, more serious, allegations emerged. The school's personnel adviser indicated that the head should see Mr Best straight away.

As soon as the strategy meeting was over, the headteacher informed the chair of governors of its outcome and sent Mr Best a note, saying that he urgently needed to speak to him about a serious matter. When Mr Best arrived in the head's office, Peter Allen told him that serious allegations had been made and that if he would like to ask a union representative to be present at the meeting, he could do so. There was a short delay while they waited for the school's union representative to arrive.

Pointing out that the allegations were of a very serious nature, the head said he had taken professional advice on how to proceed, and had been advised to read aloud to Mr Best the statements made by the two girls. He went on to do so.

 ### Statement by Sameha Mahmoud

> It all started when I was in Year 10 and Mr Best was my form teacher. There weren't enough lockers to go round and once, when Mr Best saw me carrying all my PE stuff, he said I could put my bag in his office. I was a bit upset that day because I'd had a row with my sister and when I put my bag in his room he was really kind and told me I could always talk to him if I had any problems. Then he gave me a little hug, but that was all.
>
> Over the next few weeks, I used to put my bag in his room sometimes and he'd ask me to sit down for a chat. He started saying all kinds of personal things - how his wife wasn't very nice to him and he wanted to leave her and that. Then he told me he fancied me and how I was the most attractive girl he'd ever met. I was really embarrassed and didn't know what to say, especially when he gave me a kiss on the cheek.

Anyway, this sort of thing went on until the end of term. He kept talking as if there was something going on between us and I started feeling guilty, like it was all my fault. I was hoping it would all be forgotten after the summer holidays, but when rehearsals for the school play started this term it all got worse.

The first thing that happened was that Mr Best gave me a locket. It was shaped like a heart and had "I love you" engraved on the back. He said I mustn't tell anyone he'd given it to me and should wear it under my blouse where nobody would see it. My mum and dad would have gone mad if they'd known, so I never wore it. I just hid it at the bottom of my PE bag.

One day, the rehearsal went on quite late and he asked me to stay behind after everyone else had gone. We went into his room and he told me he cared for me and asked why I kept ignoring him. I didn't say anything and he suddenly grabbed me and pressed himself up against me. I tried to get away but he was too strong. Then he kissed me on the lips. I managed to get away then and ran out of the room. I was really shocked and upset.

The next day, I told my friend Avril what had happened. She said she'd heard that Mr Best had been funny with some of the other girls in our year. Apart from Jenny Oakley, she didn't know who these girls were. So I talked to Jenny and she told me how he was always trying to grab her. He even talked her into bunking off lessons so that they could spend time together and he used to get really jealous when he saw Jenny with her boyfriend. My dad won't let me go out with boys, so I never made Mr Best jealous, but I feel sorry for Jenny because he used to shout at her and say he'd get her into trouble if she didn't chuck her boyfriend and go out with him instead.

In the end, my mum found the locket in my bag. That's when the whole story came out.

Jenny Oakley's statement was also read out. Ian Best listened to the two statements without interruption and then said, "That's absolute rubbish."

Peter Allen responded by outlining the procedures that would have to be followed. He explained that a committee of the school's Governing Body would be called to consider the allegations not less than 14 days from that day's date, and asked if Ian Best had any comments to make about the allegations. The teacher replied that the two girls had obviously allowed their imaginations to run away with them and that most of what they had said in their statements was untrue. Asked to explain what he meant, Mr Best said that he might have kissed some of the girls once or twice after rehearsals but it had all been quite innocent. "There's always a strong feeling of camaraderie in a theatrical ensemble - even an amateur one," he added.

The head now urged Mr Best to seek advice and then informed him that he was suspended on full pay and should leave the site and not return until the hearing before the governors' committee.

A few days later, Mr Best received the following letter.

Dear Mr Best,

Re: disciplinary hearing

Your attendance is requested at a disciplinary hearing to be conducted by the staffing committee of the Governing Body on Monday 28 November 2000 at 5.30 p.m. in the school library.

The purpose of the hearing is to consider the following complaints relating to your conduct:

That you committed acts of misconduct and sexual misconduct with Sameha Mahmoud, a pupil at the school, in that you:

1. Shared aspects of your personal life with her, which amounts to misconduct.
2. Used your position to make her feel guilty, which amounts to misconduct.
3. Told her you found her attractive, which amounts to misconduct.
4. Kissed her on the cheek on at least one occasion, which amounts to misconduct.
5. Gave her a locket engraved with the words "I love you", and told her not to tell anyone about the gift, which amounts to gross misconduct.
6. Cornered her in your office on 29 October 2000, pressed your body against hers and kissed her on the lips, which amounts to gross misconduct.

That you committed acts of misconduct and sexual misconduct with Jenny Oakley, a pupil at the school, in that you:

1. Gave her the key to your office, which amounts to misconduct.
2. Directed abusive language at her after seeing her speaking to a boy in her class, which amounts to misconduct.
3. Persuaded her to miss lessons in order to meet you privately, which amounts to gross misconduct.
4. Cornered her in your office on 2 November 2000 and refused to let her leave until she had let you kiss her, which amounts to gross misconduct.

The following documents will be produced in evidence at the hearing:

1. Statement by Sameha Mahmoud, Year 11 pupil
2. Statement by Mr G. Mahmoud, parent
3. Statement by Jenny Oakley, Year 11 pupil
4. Statement by Avril Hennessey, Year 11 pupil
5. Statement by Ms S. Willis, head of Year 11
6. Letter dated 17 November 2000 suspending Mr Ian Best
7. Ms Willis' notes of 15 November 2000.
8. Headteacher's notes of 17 November 2000.

In addition to myself, the following witnesses will be called:

1. Ms Sue Willis
2. Sameha Mahmoud
3. Jenny Oakley

The latter two witnesses will be accompanied by their respective parents, who will take no other part in the proceedings.

You have the right to be accompanied/represented at the hearing by an official of an independent trade union or some other person of your choice. Please let me know as soon as possible whether you will be represented at the hearing and, if so, the name and position of your representative.

Mr Roy Jones, personnel consultant, will present the school's case to the committee. The committee will be advised on legal and personnel matters by Ms Lorraine Evans.

You or your representative have the right to produce documentary evidence and to call witnesses on your behalf. Please let me have (at least four days before the hearing) the names of any witnesses you propose to call, and copies of any documents you intend to produce. A copy of the school's disciplinary procedures and the procedure to be followed at the hearing will be forwarded to you.

If you fail to attend the meeting without good cause, the committee may decide to proceed in your absence.

An additional set of documentation is enclosed for your representative.

Yours sincerely,
Peter Allen
Headteacher

Despite Ian Best's denials that he had acted improperly, and the testimony of several parents and pupils who described him as a dedicated and charismatic teacher, the governors decided to dismiss him for gross misconduct. The following statement gives their reasons.

Decision of the staff dismissal committee of the Governing Body in the disciplinary case against Ian Best

Following very careful consideration of all of the evidence, the committee has reached the unanimous decision that Mr Ian Best be dismissed from his employment at the school.

In coming to this decision, the committee has given careful consideration to all of the complaints set out in the headteacher's letter of 17 November 2000. Because of a lack of clear corroborative evidence, the committee is unable to come to a conclusion on the complaints involving Jenny Oakley.

In relation to the complaints regarding Sameha Mahmoud, the committee accepts that Mr Best gave the locket to this pupil. The giving of this gift, and in particular, the wording of the inscription, is consistent with the allegation made by Sameha Mahmoud that he had expressed affection for her, and consistent with her allegation, not denied by Mr Best, that he had kissed her in the privacy of his office. The committee therefore believes that, on the balance of probabilities, these allegations are true.

The sum total of the committee's findings is that Mr Best is guilty of gross misconduct and should be dismissed summarily from his post.

Mr Best has the right to appeal against this decision to the appeals committee of the Governing Body. If he should wish to exercise this right, he should write to the clerk to the governors at the school within 14 days of the date of this statement.

Ian Best lost his subsequent appeal against this decision. He threatened to take a claim for unfair dismissal to an employment tribunal, but his union refused to provide him with legal representation, having satisfied themselves that he had been treated fairly and that there had been no procedural irregularities in the way that the school had handled the case.

CHAPTER 5
THE ROLE OF GOVERNORS

Personnel issues in schools, including those arising from allegations of misconduct against staff, should be left to headteachers to manage on a day-to-day basis. However, education law gives the Governing Bodies of all maintained schools ultimate responsibility for managing teaching and non-teaching staff who are paid out of the school budget.

Governing Bodies are also responsible for ensuring the safety and welfare of pupils. However, in seeking to discharge this responsibility, they must take care not to infringe the rights of employees.

We strongly advise every Governing Body to make sure that it has access to personnel and legal advice and to set up a committee responsible for personnel matters. In relation to staff discipline, the personnel committee needs to ensure that the school has a code of conduct governing relations between adults and children. (A model code of conduct for school employees is included in Appendix A.) The committee should also make sure that the school adopts suitable disciplinary procedures and that these are reviewed from time to time.

Dealing with allegations against headteachers

Disciplinary matters up to and including final written warnings should normally be handled by the school's headteacher. However, where the headteacher's own conduct is the subject of an allegation by a pupil or parent, the chair of governors will need to act as the head's line manager. This means dealing with the allegations in the same way that a headteacher would do if the allegations concerned another member of staff. A summary of the procedures that need to be followed in such cases is given in the flow chart at the end of Chapter 3 of this book.

If a complaint against the headteacher is so serious that it may amount to gross misconduct justifying summary dismissal, the chair of governors must suspend the head pending further investigation and, if necessary, a hearing before the dismissal committee of the Governing Body. The decision to suspend a headteacher - or any other member of staff - should not be taken lightly. Nor can it lawfully be delegated to any person or organisation outside the school, however much pressure the police and LEA may put on governors to suspend an individual suspected of harming children. The decision to lift a suspension rests solely with the Governing Body.

Dismissal

 By law, the Governing Body must set up a staff dismissal committee with delegated powers to dismiss any member of staff whose conduct is found to be unacceptable. The Governing Body is also required to set up a separate appeals committee with delegated powers to hear an appeal against dismissal.

Each committee must be made up of at least three members, and governors involved in a decision to dismiss a member of staff should not hear an appeal against that decision.

Where a headteacher's dismissal is under consideration, the chair of governors will almost certainly have investigated allegations concerning the head's conduct and so should not sit either on the dismissal or appeals committee.

If a headteacher or other member of staff has been dismissed for misconduct involving children or young people, or has resigned to avoid dismissal, the Governing Body must inform the Secretary of State for Education and Employment. The Secretary of State may then bar that person from working with children or young people in future.

APPENDIX A

A MODEL CODE OF CONDUCT FOR STAFF EMPLOYED IN SCHOOLS

The following model code of conduct should be seen as a starting point, which schools may wish to expand and develop for their own use.

1. Purpose

1.1 This code of conduct is intended to reduce the risk of false or malicious allegations of misconduct by pupils and students against staff. It will be appreciated, however, that the code of conduct cannot totally remove that risk.

1.2 This code should be read in conjunction with the school's child protection procedures, with which staff must be familiar.

2. Relationships with pupils

2.1 The relationship between an employee and a pupil is a formal one, and an appropriate 'distance' should always be maintained. Teachers, in particular, are important role models and should conduct themselves accordingly. Employees must take care that the age, sex, maturity and cultural background of the pupils is taken into consideration in their relationships with pupils. Employees must be alert to the possibility that pupils may misinterpret, deliberately or innocently, adult behaviour or language and should be vigilant in this respect. Excessively informal or ambiguous language, or behaviour which may be interpreted as intimidatory or physically threatening should be avoided. Sarcastic, demeaning or insensitive comments towards pupils, and haranguing and aggressive shouting are abusive and therefore unacceptable.

3. Physical contact

3.1 Any circumstance where physical contact is used increases the vulnerability of the employee. Physical contact is rarely appropriate or acceptable and must be avoided. It may, rarely, be appropriate for a member of staff to use physical restraint or intervention in order to prevent a pupil causing injury or harm to him/herself or others or damaging property. This must always be the minimum force required and the incident must always be reported.

3.2   Teachers of subjects where physical contact may occasionally be necessary, such as physical education or drama, should endeavour to demonstrate particular techniques by using competent pupils. Where the teacher uses physical contact, the contact should be planned and explained to pupils and must be demonstrably unavoidable.

3.3   Physical contact may be necessary where there is a life threatening or serious condition. Employees who administer first aid should ensure that, wherever possible, other children or another adult are present.

4. Corporal punishment

4.1   The law forbids a teacher to use any degree of physical contact which is deliberately intended to punish a pupil, or which is primarily intended to cause pain, injury or humiliation. This includes interference with a pupil's body or clothes, for example, shaking or holding the pupil by the lapels of his or her jacket.

5. Private meetings

5.1   Private meetings must be avoided. Where such a meeting is demonstrably unavoidable, then it must take place in an appropriate room with the door left open and/or with visual contact with others maintained. The use of 'Meeting in Progress' signs is inappropriate.

5.2   Under no circumstances should meetings with individual pupils be arranged off the school premises, or on the school premises when the school is not in session, without the prior approval of the headteacher or a senior colleague with delegated authority to approve such meetings. This includes the transporting of individual children in private cars.

6. Pupils with special educational needs

6.1   Employees should seek specific guidance from their line manager in relation to pupils with special needs who require assistance with personal needs such as toiletting.

7. Infatuations and crushes

7.1 Infatuations and crushes can involve pupils and staff of both sexes on both a heterosexual and homosexual basis. An employee in such a situation should inform a senior colleague without delay. The situation must be taken seriously and the member of staff should be careful to ensure that no encouragement of any kind is given to the pupil. Careless and insensitive reactions may provoke false accusations. Young, newly qualified teachers must recognise their particular vulnerability to adolescent infatuation.

8. Out-of-school and after-school activities

8.1 Staff should take particular care when supervising pupils, especially older pupils, in the less formal atmosphere of a residential setting, school holiday or out-of-school activity. The more relaxed relationships that may promote successful activities can be misinterpreted by young people. The standards of professional conduct and behaviour expected of employees are no different to those which apply when the school is in session.

9. Teaching and teaching materials

9.1 Teaching and teaching materials must be appropriate, having regard to the age, understanding and cultural background of the pupils concerned. The use of material such as books, videos and films of an explicit or sensitive nature, particularly in relation to language or sexual behaviour, must be given careful consideration to ensure that its selection is not subsequently misinterpreted. There should always, therefore, be a clear link with the targets of the teacher's planning. The content of lessons must also comply with the school's policy on sex and relationship education.

10. Reporting incidents

10.1 Staff must report any concerns that they may have following any incident where they feel that their actions may have been misinterpreted, or where a pupil, parent or third party has complained to them either about their own actions or the actions of another member of staff.

APPENDIX B
USEFUL ADDRESSES

Advisory Conciliation and Arbitration Service
ACAS Head Office
Brandon House
180 Borough High Street
London SE1 1LW
Telephone: 020 7396 5100 (Customer Enquiry Line for London region)
For most enquiries, contact your own regional office (under Dept of Trade and Industry)

Chartered Institute of Personnel and Development
35 Camp Road
London SW19 4UX
Telephone: 020 8971 9000 (ask for enquiries)
website: www.ipd.co.uk (accessible to non-members)

Education Personnel Management Ltd
St John's House
Spitfire Close
Ermine Business Park
Huntingdon
Cambs. PE18 6EP
Telephone: 01480 431993
Fax: 01480 431992
e-mail: epm@educ-personnel.co.uk
website: www.epm.co.uk

National Association of Governors and Managers (NAGM)
Suite 1, 4th Floor
Western House
Smallbrook Queensway
Birmingham B5 4HQ
Telephone/Fax: 0121 643 5787
e-mail: governorhq@hotmail.com
website: www.nagm.org.uk

National Governors Council
Glebe House
Church Street
Crediton
Devon EX17 2AF
Telephone: 01363 774377
Fax: 01363 776007
e-mail: ngc@ngc.org.uk
website: www.ngc.org.uk

National Society for the Prevention of Cruelty to Children
NSPCC National Centre
42 Curtain Road
London EC2A 3NH
Telephone: 020 7825 2500
Fax: 020 7825 2525
website: www.nspcc.org.uk

THE EDUCATION PERSONNEL MANAGEMENT SERIES

Managing Allegations Against Staff is the fourth handbook in the series. Other titles include:

BOOK 1 THE WELL TEACHER
promoting staff health, beating stress and reducing absence

by Maureen Cooper

ISBN: 1-85539-058-2

Gives clear management strategies for promoting staff health, beating stress and reducing staff absence. Stress is not peculiar to staff in education, but is a common cause of absence. Large amounts of limited school budgets are spent each year on sick pay and supply cover. This book gives straightforward practical advice on how to deal strategically with health issues through proactively promoting staff health. It includes suggestions for reducing stress levels in schools. It also outlines how to deal with individual cases of staff absence.

BOOK 2 MANAGING CHALLENGING PEOPLE
dealing with staff conduct

by Maureen Cooper and Bev Curtis

ISBN: 1-85539-057-4

This handbook deals with managing staff whose conduct gives cause for concern. It summarises the employment relationships in schools and those areas of education and employment law relevant to staff discipline. It looks at the difference between conduct and capability, and misconduct and gross misconduct, and describes disciplinary and dimissal procedures relating to teaching and non-teaching staff and headteachers.

BOOK 3 MANAGING POOR PERFORMANCE
handling staff capability issues

by Maureen Cooper and Bev Curtis

ISBN: 1-85539-062-0

This handbook explains clearly why capability is important, and gives advice on how to identify staff with poor performance and how to help them improve. It outlines the legal position and the role of governors, and details the various stages of formal capability procedures and dismissal hearings. The book provides model letters to use and is illustrated by real-life case studies. This provides the help you need to give you confidence in tackling these difficult issues.

Other Network Educational Press Publications

THE SCHOOL EFFECTIVENESS SERIES

Book 1: *Accelerated Learning in the Classroom* by Alistair Smith
ISBN: 1-85539-034-5
- The first book in the UK to apply new knowledge about the brain to classroom practice
- Contains practical methods so teachers can apply accelerated learning theories to their own classrooms
- Aims to increase the pace of learning and deepen understanding
- Includes advice on how to create the ideal environment for learning and how to help learners fulfil their potential
- Full of lively illustrations, diagrams and plans
- Offers practical solutions on improving performance, motivation and understanding
- Contains a checklist of action points for the classroom - 21 ways to improve learning

Book 2: *Effective Learning Activities* by Chris Dickinson
ISBN: 1-85539-035-3
- An essential teaching guide which focuses on practical activities to improve learning
- Aims to improve results through effective learning, which will raise achievement, deepen understanding, promote self-esteem and improve motivation
- Includes activities which are designed to promote differentiation and understanding
- Offers advice on how to maximise the use of available - and limited - resources
- Includes activities suitable for GCSE, National Curriculum, Highers, GSVQ and GNVQ
- From the author of the highly acclaimed *Differentiation: A Practical Handbook of Classroom Strategies*

Book 3: *Effective Heads of Department* by Phil Jones and Nick Sparks
ISBN: 1-85539-036-1
- An ideal support for Heads of Department looking to develop necessary management skills
- Contains a range of practical systems and approaches; each of the eight sections ends with a 'checklist for action'
- Designed to develop practice in line with OFSTED expectations and DfEE thinking by monitoring and improving quality
- Addresses issues such as managing resources, leadership, learning, departmental planning and making assessment valuable
- Includes useful information for Senior Managers in schools who are looking to enhance the effectiveness of their Heads of Department

Book 4: *Lessons are for Learning* by Mike Hughes
ISBN: 1-85539-038-8
- Brings together the theory of learning with the realities of the classroom environment
- Encourages teachers to reflect on their own classroom practice and challenges them to think about why they teach in the way they do
- Develops a clear picture of what constitutes effective classroom practice
- Offers practical suggestions for activities that bridge the gap between recent developments in the theory of learning and the constraints of classroom teaching
- Ideal for stimulating thought and generating discussion
- Written by a practising teacher who has also worked as a teaching advisor, a PGCE co-ordinator and an OFSTED inspector

Book 5:   *Effective Learning in Science* by Paul Denley and Keith Bishop
ISBN: 1-85539-039-6
- A book that looks at planning for effective learning within the context of science
- Encourages discussion about the aims and purposes in teaching science and the role of subject knowledge in effective teaching
- Tackles issues such as planning for effective learning, the use of resources and other relevant management issues
- Offers help in development of a departmental plan to revise schemes of work, resources, classroom strategies, in order to make learning and teaching more effective
- Ideal for any science department aiming to increase performance and improve results

Book 6:   *Raising Boys' Achievement* by Jon Pickering
ISBN: 1-85539-040-X
- Addresses the causes of boys' under-achievement and offers possible solutions
- Focuses the search for causes and solutions on teachers working in the classroom
- Looks at examples of good practice in schools to help guide the planning and implementation of strategies to raise achievement
- Offers practical, 'real' solutions, along with tried and tested training suggestions
- Ideal as a basis for INSET or as a guide to practical activities for classroom teachers

Book 7:   *Effective Provision for Able and Talented Children* by Barry Teare
ISBN: 1-85539-041-8
- Basic theory, necessary procedures and turning theory into practice
- Main methods of identifying the able and talented
- Concerns about achievement and appropriate strategies to raise achievement
- The role of the classroom teacher, monitoring and evaluation techniques
- Practical enrichment activities and appropriate resources

Book 8:   *Effective Careers Education & Guidance* by Andrew Edwards and
Anthony Barnes
ISBN: 1-85539-045-0
- Strategic planning of the careers programme as part of the wider curriculum
- Practical consideration of managing careers education and guidance
- Practical activities for reflection and personal learning, and case studies where such activities have been used
- Aspects of guidance and counselling involved in helping students to understand their own capabilities and form career plans
- Strategies for reviewing and developing existing practice

Book 9:   *Best behaviour and Best Behaviour FIRST AID* by Peter Relf, Rod Hirst, Jan Richardson and
Georgina Youdell
ISBN: 1-85539-046-9
- Provides support for those who seek starting points for effective behaviour management, for individual teachers and for middle and senior managers
- Focuses on practical and useful ideas for individual schools and teachers

Best Behaviour FIRST AID
ISBN: 1-85539-047-7
- Provides strategies to cope with aggression, defiance and disturbance
- Straightforward action points for self-esteem

Book 10:   *The Effective School Governor* by David Marriott
ISBN: 1-85539-042-6
- Straightforward guidance on how to fulfil a governor's role and responsibilities
- Develops your personal effectiveness as an individual governor
- Practical support on how to be an effective member of the governing team
- Audio tape for use in car or at home

Book 11:   *Improving Personal Effectiveness for Managers in Schools* by James Johnson
ISBN: 1-85539-049-3
- An invaluable resource for new and experienced teachers in both primary and secondary schools
- Contains practical strategies for improving leadership and management skills
- Focuses on self-management skills, managing difficult situations, working under pressure, developing confidence, creating a team ethos and communicating effectively

Book 12:   *Making Pupil Data Powerful* by Maggie Pringle and Tony Cobb
ISBN: 1-85539-053-3
- Shows teachers in primary, middle and secondary schools how to interpret pupils' performance data and how to use it to enhance teaching and learning
- Provides practical advice on analysing performance and learning behaviours, measuring progress, predicting future attainment, setting targets and ensuring continuity and progression
- Explains how to interpret national initiatives on data-analysis, benchmarking and target-setting, and to ensure that these have value in the classroom

Book 13:   *Closing the Learning Gap* by Mike Hughes
ISBN: 1-85539-051-5
- Help teachers, departments and schools to close the Learning Gap between what we know about effective learning and what actually goes on in the classroom
- Encourages teachers to reflect on ways in which they teach, and to identify and implement strategies for improving their practice
- Full of practical advice and real, tested strategies for improvement
- Written by a teacher, for teachers, to stimulate thought and interest 'at a glance'

Book 14:   *Getting Started: an induction guide for Newly Qualified Teachers* by Henry Liebling
ISBN: 1-85539-054-X
- An induction guide for newly qualified teachers giving advice on their first year of teaching - how to get to know the school and their new pupils, how to work with their induction tutor and when to ask for help
- Includes masses of practical advice on issues such as getting to grips with the school's documentation, managing pupils' behaviour, time management, classroom management and dealing with tiredness and stress
- Draws on the author's extensive experience as a lecturer and teacher trainer
- Gives NQTs guidance on what to look for when observing experienced colleagues, how to evaluate and develop their own teaching, and to build on their Career Entry Profile to meet the requirements of the induction standards
- Provides an overview of theories in teaching and learning styles, models of teaching, and teaching and learning strategies

OTHER PUBLICATIONS

Imagine that... by Stephen Bowkett
> ISBN: 1-85539-043-4
> - Hands on, user-friendly manual for stimulating creative thinking, talking and writing in the classroom
> - Provides over 100 practical and immediately useable classroom activities and games that can be used in isolation, or in combination, to help meet the requirements and standards of the National Curriculum
> - Explores the nature of creative thinking and how this can be effectively driven through an ethos of positive encouragement, mutual support and celebration of success and achievement
> - Empowers children to learn how to learn

Helping with Reading by Anne Butterworth and Angela White
> ISBN: 1-95539-044-2
> - Includes sections on 'Hearing Children Read', 'Word Recognition' and 'Phonics'
> - Provides precisely focused, easily implemented follow-up activities for pupils who need extra reinforcement of basic reading skills
> - Activities which directly relate to the National Curriculum and 'Literacy Hour' group work. They are clear, practical and easily implemented. Ideas and activities can also be incorporated into Individual Education Plans.
>
> - Aims to address current concerns about reading standards and to provide support in view of the growing use of classroom assistants and parents to help with the teaching of reading

Self Intelligence by Stephen Bowkett
> ISBN: 1-85539-055-8
> - Designed to help explore and develop emotional resourcesfulness in yourself and the children you teach
> - High self-esteem underpins success in education. More broadly, emotionaly resourcefulness results in improved behaviour and higher standards

Effective Resources for Able and Talented Children by Barry Teare
> ISBN: 1-85539-050-7
> - Sequel to *Effective Provisions for Able and Talented Children*
> - Provides photocopiable resources for Key Stages 2 and 3
> - Arranged into 4 themes: Literacy, Mathematics/Numeracy, Science, Humanities

THE ACCELERATED LEARNING SERIES

Book 1 :   *Accelerated Learning in Practice* by Alistair Smith
ISBN: 1-85539-048-5
- The author's second book which takes Nobel Prize winning brain research into the classroom
- Structured to help readers access and retain the information neccessary to begin to accelerate their own learning and that of the students they teach
- Contains over 100 learning tools and case studies from 36 schools
- Includes 9 principles of learning based on brain research and the author's Seven Stage Accelerated Learning Cycle

Book 2 :   *The Alps Approach: Accelerated Leraning in Primary Schools* by Alistair Smith and Nicola Call
ISBN: 1-85539-056-6
- Takes research collected by Alistair Smith and shows how it can be used to great effect in the primary classroom
- Provides practical and accessible examples of strategies used at a UK primary school where SATs results shot up as a consequence
- Gives readers the opportunity to develop the alps approach for themselves and for children in their care

Book 3 :   *Mapwise: Accelerated Learning Through Visible Thinking* by Oliver Caviglioli and Ian Harris
ISBN: 1-85539-059-0
- This book aims at improving thinking skills through teacher explanation and pupil understanding, and so improves your school's capacity for learning
- Makes teacher planning, teaching and reviewing easier and more effective
- Brilliantly illustrated, it offers the most effective means of addressing the National Curriculum thinking skills requirements by infusing thinking into subject teaching